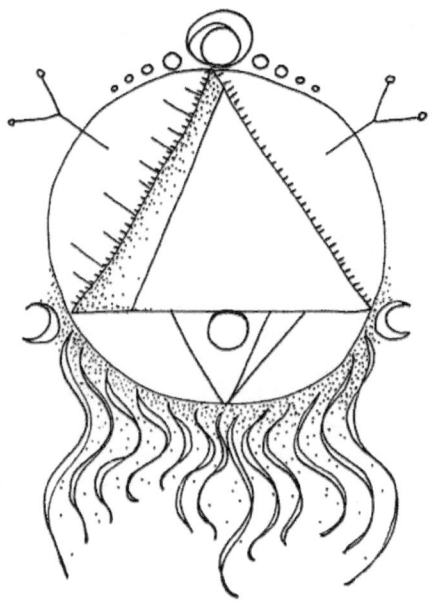

In the deepest sense, we all dream
not of ourselves, but out of what lies
between us and the other.

~ Carl G. Jung

The day is coming
when a single carrot,
freshly observed,
will set off a revolution.

~ Paul Cézanne

Yes Before Breakfast Press
2019
All Rights Reserved

Deep Low Bow
Poems & Stories of Impermanence & Love

by

Enza Marie
Putignano

(Top Shelf)

And then there is this,
the gentle openness of
a high, forgiving kiss.
Our stainless, lucid
courage as we
turn yet another
crisp, clean page
to meet the edge.

One single drop
may cause the
rain barrel
to overflow.
It doesn't
mean it's
the fault
of
this
one
single
drop.

(Alms)

I thought I heard you
late last night throwing
lost rocks at my window,
but I couldn't be sure,
so, I painted it shut,
dirt-blood-red,
and left the brush
to dry on the ledge.

Then I snuck a peak
out the back door
where I saw an old
woman in a yellow dress.
She was putting out food
for the cats and the dogs,
the wake and the fog,
my holding, my distress.

"Have you seen your wild?"
she asked, silver fox flashing past.

Secret of our basic goodness
pooling me steady to receive.
Saffron-gold soul, fluid as
a Tibetan robe, filling
my empty bowl.
Gonging me
to trust.

(True Blue)

Dear Oxygen,

I know I haven't
written in a while.
I'm sorry.
I've been stuck
just outside
Heaven and Hell,
the gases here
thinner,
farther reaching,
but yesterday
I remembered
how we
used
to
wake
up
together
and dive
deeply into
each other's
eyes before going
on with our day.

(Got a Light?)

I ran into my subconscious at the diner last night. She was smoking a *Gauloise* like it was 1969, florescent chrome and glass framing her mild side. We sat in silence for a while, but she never looked me in the eye.

When I ordered the last piece of apple pie à la mode, she got all mad and started sulking, going on about last Wednesday, something I'd said at the recycle center. I couldn't really understand. We tried Google translate, but everything has its limits.

Then, my "other-mother" walked in, followed by my favorite teacher with the strawberry blonde braids, my taciturn boyfriend from the seventh grade and my wily boss from high caste Ubud with his three-legged, tiger-striped dog.

Too bad the bathroom was out of order.

My subconscious quickly moved to a planet on my left.

"Come, everyone," I said, "I'll share my pie."

(Trick or Treat)

When words aren't enough
and mountains separate,
when ether is all we have,
I put on my space helmet
and sparkling silver sneakers
and pretend it's Halloween.
Every day filling my bag.

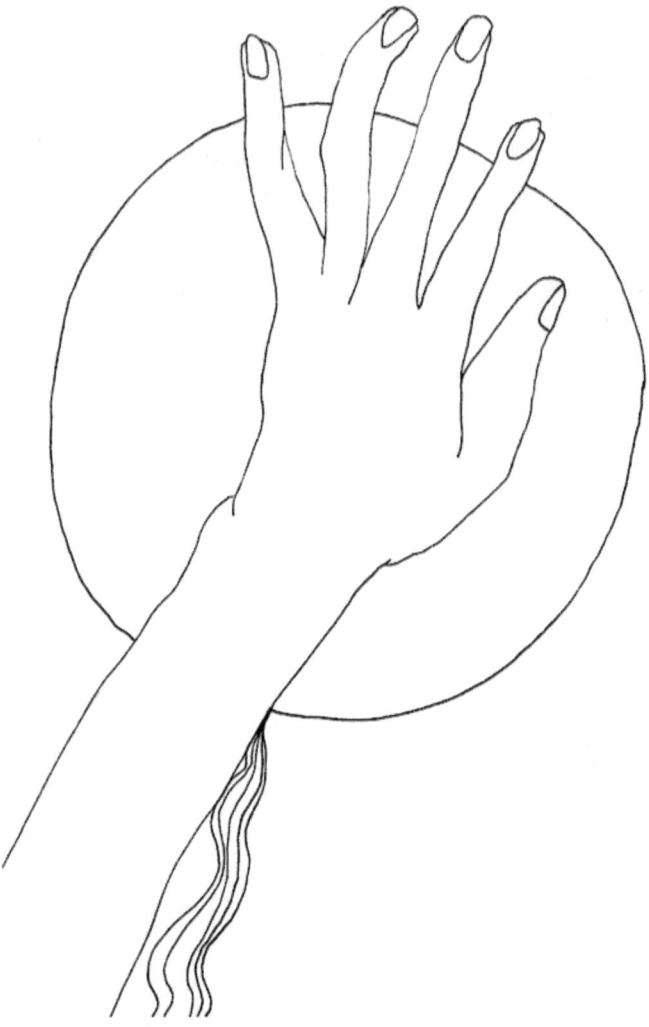

(Usherance)

I went to the movies alone
and sat on the side, in the back,
putting my thin stockinged feet up
above my head. I looked around for you,
but you weren't there, though the seat before
me sagged deep burgundy with preview and
warmth. Up on the screen lightening flashed,
while mist and hope rained down upon our faces
blue. Embracing ourselves to death. Jump cut to
hot coffee, pre-dawn redemption breakfast, eggs
over easy. Action soft and slow. Then the boom
of the credits, surrounding sound returning me
to real. It took me a while to find my shoes.
I'd gone a long way off. Popcorn and
caramel stuck in my teeth, sugar
coating all I cannot reach.
Favorite slate gray
mitten lost.

(PleaseMoveOverPlease)

Don't be afraid when you draw
the Sorrow card, she just wants to
be held, to have her hair smoothed,
the back of her neck gently kissed.
She just wants to take up a little more
room in the bed, to have the candles lit,
the music fine-tuned. Zippers and snaps
and scarves and socks peeled back to the
lunar pulse of her vast nakedness.

Don't be afraid when you draw the
Sorrow card, for this undulation
within, this nest you create, offers
you the melt of attention you need.

Don't be afraid.

Our sadness knows our greatest smile,
set inside our liberation to be real.

Yes.

Make great space for Sorrow as
she slides her vibrating, watery trail
across plump pillows of distraction
to fling the covers back, lean in
real close, tuck us into grace.

(Compass)

Somewhere
beyond the gale,
phosphorescent shadows
slink home,
holes at the knees,
and I greet them, with a
cup of steaming-hot trust,
at the gate.

(One-Way Ticket)

Dear Anxiety,

I thought
if I closed
all the windows
and locked the doors
you wouldn't find me
sliding the terraced edge,
mud and wet grasses
teasing my skirted knees, the
bullshit of my sweat-stained calm.
But there you were, as
I poured golden butter
oil from a slick-sided jar,
slipping prized calories
to the trash.
Hammering
velvet nails.
Heavy twine
repairing.
Monster
trucks
parked
every
which
way
in
the
drive.

(Never-Never Land)

Do you remember
swinging in trees,
knees rough
and green,
arms free,
exploring,
sunlight soaring,
soft belly exposed,
possibility whole,
everything
hanging
in balance?
Did you imagine
then, in a layering
of glue and
feathers and
felt, that one day
you may rewrite
this dream?
That one day
you may
abandon
wind?

(Spelunking)

And then he said to me, "What is it you're afraid of?"

And I said, "I'm afraid I'll run out of space.

"I'm afraid I'll remain afraid of running out of space and will forever create yellow and black striped barriers in my irony of mind. I'm afraid I'll never understand that the way I feel will change, on the surface, every damn day, but that below this, tropical sea divers, calm fish, orange and pink, will continuously swim to kiss my forehead, opening my third eye wide behind my softly steaming mask.

"And too, I'm afraid that when I'm afraid, I'll drop a guillotine on you, only it will come down hard and heavy on my left foot and I'll hop, hop, hop around in circles, distracted in one direction, looking back over my shoulder trying to create balance. Yeah, I'm afraid of that.

"I'm afraid I'll remain an apology."

Then I left, popped across the street to the convenience store and wandered without wonder, every aisle the same. Self-conscious florescence, polysorbate 80 and DDT. Bright metallic blues and greens promising us nothing we truly need. I bought a big water.

When I came outside with my offering, there he was in the parking lot beneath a wobbly circle of light, leaning lanky decades upon a splintered pole, softly strumming his heart out, singing about a jack rabbit on his back until his voice cracked.

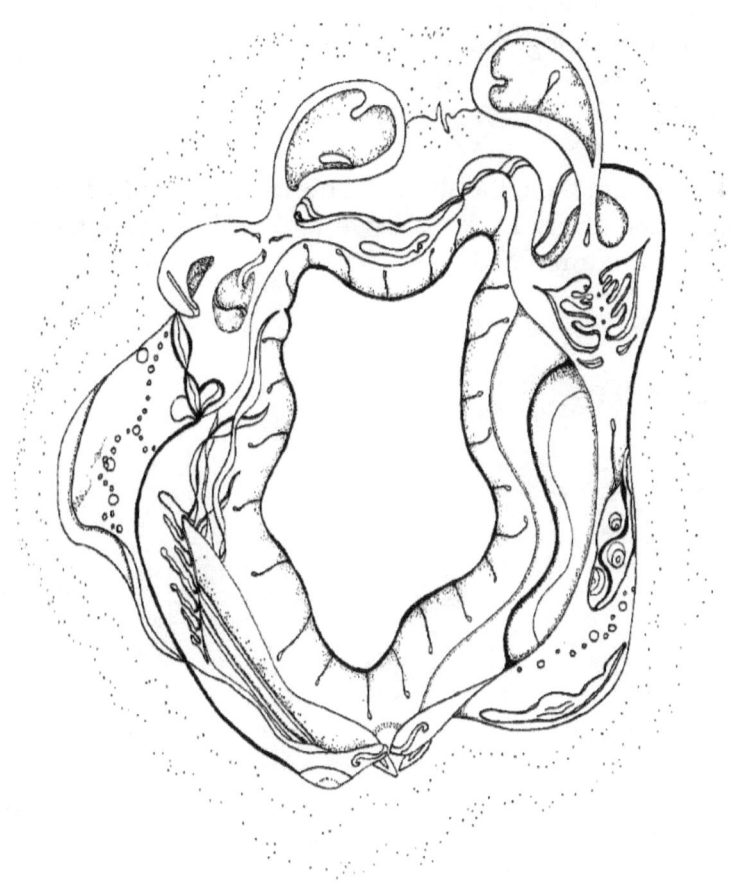

Together, we laughed and laughed.

Then I said, "Let's go now, under the blooming grapefruit tree where we can sit together. Really see one another."

And we did.

And I kissed him then, the shame at his temple, and he kissed mine at the nape of my neck. And we took in long breaths, as our fears danced illuminated.

(Shake It Up)

If I could I would
shrink you to fit inside
a crystal snow globe at your desk.

Only it wouldn't be a snow globe, it
would be a deep beach-bowl. A golden-
pink and sandy hold of warm and salty
sea, foaming and jumping, awake as
your sister's Rice Krispies surfing a
sweet milk wave when you were eight.

Around the edges mini palm trees would
shimmy and sway, shimmy and sway, tickling
bold nose holes of those who come sniffing
around your desk looking for work.

Oh! Don't you worry.
I've got you covered.
I've been to school.
I know the type.

They won't be able to see you anyway,
swinging in your soft cotton hammock
beneath the sweep of a perfect banana
grove. Purple-black, silver-red, tear-shaped
bud knocking you once, gently, upon the
head, reminding you there's nowhere to go.

Later while you're sleeping, I'll reach
my old enormity down and stroke
your dog-eared feet with my pinky.

And you'll remember that endless summer
you fell in love with your best friend's brother.

I'll whisper then, calling in the dolphins and
whales from their whirling emerald cove, and
you'll rest and play, rest and play, until you're
ready. Ready once again for crystal snow.

(So Within)

Last night I decided to follow the street sweeper home. She'd had a very busy "day" sweeping up after all the spirit revelers and people of consciousness reflecting upon what had been, what's still to come.

You should've seen the piles. Loneliness and fear heaped upon ripe and leaky faith. Hopelessness and trust sliding through ideas of new homes, recovered lost-love and angry bosses. Accomplishment crunching in beside barefoot persuasion. Attachment. Righteous bravado.

Turns out the street sweeper lives underground. No real surprise. As I followed, I kept a cool distance, dodging yellow pools of light and weaving gutters, empty as faded dreams, though whispering the momentum of a clear, tiny stream.

Staying upwind of my sweeper was key. It seems that her tending to all that purging cleanses her from within. She smelled amazing, like a wild garden of medicinal plants and night-blooming flowers. The moisture in the air made me want to rub her back, run my fingers through her hair.

By the time we reached the dunes, the sun was just peeking over the tops of the fringy hills. In a flash she dropped down into her hole and I dropped cautiously behind, sliding two stories to arrive on solid ground.

Looking around, I realized she was nowhere to be found.

Before me were several passageways from which to choose. I shut my eyes, reached out my arm and spun round. Then I went straight. The tunnel was well lit, and high, no need to squat or crawl. The air was fine. A bright amber glow gave the sandy enclosure a comfortable sense of hearth and home.

When the tunnel spilled out onto a vaulted chamber, again I was not surprised. There in the center was a grand table of mahogany wood filled with the many sweepers of the world, their deep bowls piled high with the narrow ideals and projections that keep those above divided. The sweepers were laughing and sighing, slathering the funky stuff up with honey and dew while reaching long, spindly limbs across the warm space to feed one another and coo.

Of course, I couldn't help but to GASP OUT LOUD.

They all turned and saw me then, the littlest of them, my own sweet sweeper, getting up swiftly to dance to the "corner" and get me a broom.

Dance to the corner of a circular room....

Get me a broom.

(SPF 50)

Dear Romance,

What a surprise it was
seeing you at the beach
on Saturday, all kicked back,
with your new, still red, classic
tattoo: *Ouroboros*, a snake eating its
tail. You, alone, taking in the rosy sink
and glow of another day's sacred close.

And, OH! I love what you've done with your hair.
That's your natural color, isn't it?

After I got home, I was reminded
of that February in Miami, when
we stole that leaky rowboat.
Neither
of
us
able
to keep
our balance for long.

Reminded of that time my
whole fell into the canal and I dove
in after it, after the perfect ripple of us.

My lungs have never quite been the same.
I coughed for nearly two years after-
ward to clear it all away.

Finally, I moved to the high

desert. I liked it there, the psychic
space of it. The heat and dry.
Rent was cheap, too.
And with cosmos in my garden and
a dog called *Solidad*. She passed last
month. I buried her in the red earth
of Eagle's Point. Laying her body to
rest with mop heads, sneakers and
bones. Eternal, tender buffet.

Anyway,
I'm super glad
we crossed paths.
I almost didn't recognize you.

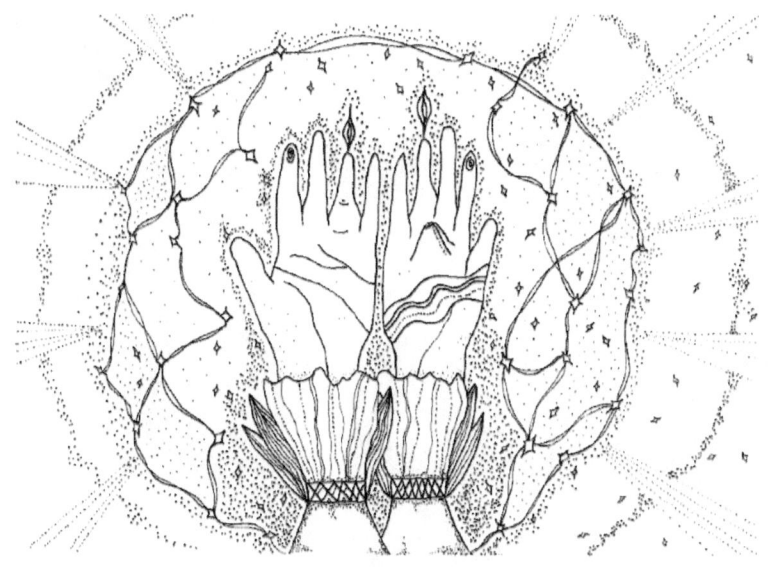

(General Delivery)

I dreamt you sent me a love letter.
It came to me in the jungle,
amidst thick, raucous vines
and weeping mosses.
It arrived flat,
atop a stack,
translucent skin
punctuated with
tiny, perfect
holes,
like stars.
So fragile.
There was
a photograph, too.
In it you were smiling
and pointing
somewhere
beyond.
I was tickled.
Shy. Excited.
A summer-camp
pen pal as I read
your letter.
Just then,
a crab skittered
by, making her
way home.

(RSVP)

I thought it was going to be the gathering of the year, but of all those I invited, only Anxiety, Uncertainty and Compassion showed up. I knew I should've gone with Saturday rather than Tuesday night. Though maybe it was my directions.

Anxiety arrived first, before I'd finished putting out the hors d'oeuvres. Ripe cheese, salty nuts and figs from the backyard. Anx was dressed all in black: skinny jeans, tight boat neck, trench and sash. After lining up their soft-soled shoes and hanging their coat carefully over the back of an Eames knockoff, Anx followed me tentatively to the kitchen, offering to help carry out the last of the trays. They said they were vegan, so would only carry things I'd prepared *sans animals*. I turned the music up and casually sent Anx to the patio to check the fire.

Next up, Uncertainty. I was so hoping Un would come. Every other time I'd invited them, they didn't show. Goodness, what an outfit! Zebra stripes and snakeskin boots, a 1940s smoking jacket and pearls. I was thrilled to have Un at my table, though slightly edgy. When would the others arrive?

Anx, Un and I opened the champagne and raised a glass to the future. Un downed theirs and threw the glass into the fire. Anx went inside to change the music.

I think we were all relieved when the doorbell rang and Compassion entered, a large, supple satchel over their shoulder. They opened it onto the patio, spilling out an African savannah, the Milky Way, Puerto Rico, the fish market in Cannes.... We gasped.

Compassion wanted us all to dance, but Uncertainty and Anxiety were already deep in discussion, standing before the dining room mirror. I said I would, just needed a minute to change. "Oh, don't change," Com said. Still, I ran to my room and put on my favorite coral reef dress. I wasn't sure it could withstand the swirling, fragile as it'd become, but it was my favorite and I felt really good with Com.

Compassion sure knew how to tango. I knew a little. What a divine and connected language. Com was a great teacher, never stopped smiling and holding eye contact. Dipping and twirling me like I was air.

Uncertainty and Anxiety had elevated their talk to the roof, though it took a bit of convincing on A.'s part.

The savannah had moved into the bathroom and Puerto Rico took up on the kitchen counter. I really wanted to try a bit of the Milky Way, but Compassion discouraged me, saying, "Yes, I hear you. Yes, it *is* super appealing and mysterious and right there before you, yet it's an entity unto itself, not yours to consume, my dear."

"Thank you," I said, and kissed their cheek.

I called a cab for A. and U., who clearly would be leaving together. Then I drank a big glass of water at the sink and went to offer one to C., but they were already asleep, curled up like a fallen leaf in the palm of my outstretched hand.

(Leftovers)

Dear Expectation,

I thought you were coming over last night,
didn't you say you were coming over?

After I saw you on the corner, my arms weighed down
with onions and potatoes, beet greens, tomatoes,
and we stood there, a boiling pot,
didn't you say you were?

It's like we live in a world with no absolutes,
only then we don't, cuz we do, you know?

Or don't you?

I can pretend to know,
to sip the hot, self-satisfied soup,
but I think I'll go to the Indian buffet instead.

Maybe I will, maybe I won't, see you there....

(Headwaters)

Remember that time you climbed the tree of my no-longer-childhood after bouncing soft-rock inquiries through the open pane of my window? Me, waiting for the sound of you clinking tiny pieces of yourself gathered from the debris at the side of the road.

Imagined rain-washed majesty. Pristine mountaintop. Toss. Chink. *Clink.*

Yes. Yes, you do. You remember. Like it was yesterday, only today.

Do you remember the river rush? Turbulent jade procession flooding the top of the very tree you climbed, thinking I was you. The river lifting us up above the forest to our bed of silent dreams.

And that time, before the river came, sitting together upon cool roof slates. *Ouija* board balancing our up- turned, out-turned, earth-known knees. Innocence squeezed. Questions hanging, indigo, upon the early evening breeze.

Growing depth of us suspended in a quiver of fingertips.

Sly, adolescent heave of chest sweeping our small town, our sleepy hold, our bare, dusty, moon-kissed souls of gold. Our New Fate. New Ideals.

Oh, yes, you remember. I know. For, my darling, we reap what we sow. Reap what we sow.

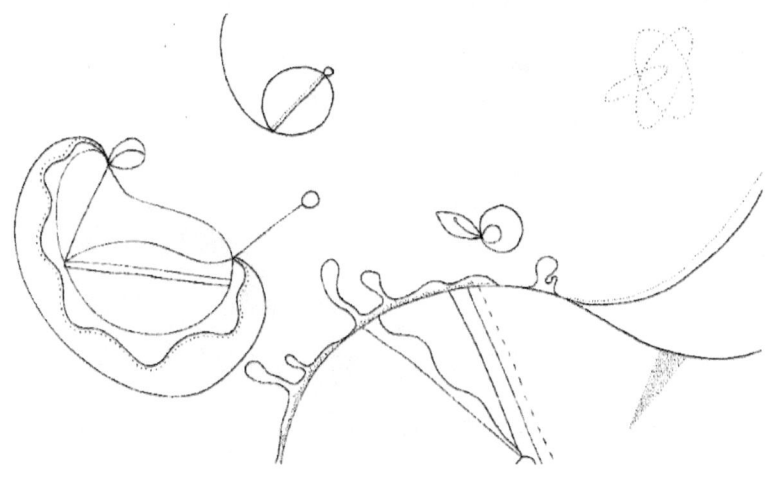

(All Aboard)

Did you notice the fence fell
down in the back yard?

Now we can't look at each
other through island-shaped holes.

If you want, I can use my floppy
old hat to float across the gap.

I'll lay it down at my smoothest
shore and step in like a cat,
come over to pick you up.

Don't forget to leave your
good shoes at home.

(Blend Well)

Will you
make cookies with me?
I left my past out
all night in a deep,
star-dusted bowl
my grandmother passed
on to me from her grandmother,
from her grandmother. I left it out
on top the fridge
all night, so it
could soften.
We can blend
it with the silken bag
of dreams I've been collecting.
I finally went through them this
dark moon and threw the moldy ones
to the chickens behind the house.
They got drunk.
Then were silent for hours.
For weeks now I've been gathering
rich, pungent seeds, drawn in
on waves of *"Yes."*
They sing to me.
I was thinking we
could leave our cookies
raw. What do you think?
Will you please bring a box of awakening?
Your bright red action extract? Mine turned a
kind of dry-grass yellow. Maybe the neighbors
have some salt of the Earth we can borrow.
Already, the fires are burning.
Come whenever you can.

(One Size Fits All)

I received a collect call from Courage Cowardice this morning.

"Will you accept the charges?" said a voice, sleepy with indifference and the smell of day-old doughnuts.

Though my guts churned, my inquiring mind wanted to "know," and so, "Yes," I said, "I'll accept the charges."

The receiver was hot and heavy in my hand, 1,001 open wormholes pressing my ear with silence.

"Yes, indeed. Reverse the charges," I said. "Hello? Courage Cowardice? Are you there?"

Flick. Womp. Slam.

From the other end I heard running, heavy across a slick grey floor.

Skid. Screeeeech.

Gasp.

"I've been so busy, so busy, you know. I had to dig to China, jump my custom-built motorbike over Niagara Falls, cross the Great Bering Strait in a teacup... I'm sorry, I'm sorry I didn't call, I'm sorry I abandoned you at Disneyland with that six-shooter, my shrink, and my ex. I've been so busy, so busy, you know," said Courage Cowardice. "Raincheck? Raincheck? Are you free Wednesday? No, not Wednesday. What about Friday? Friday next? Can I pick you up? Maybe we can get a tattoo."

Wow. Courage Cowardice was calling me collect. Again. To apologize for *missing their alarm*.

I told them I'd think about a date, but that I had friends in town, no one they knew. Yes, I'd take them up on their neon rain check, meet them at the top of the Empire State Building, naked, at dawn, to talk about our shit, but that if they didn't show, I'd have to empty their locker, take the superhero costumes I'd made for them, and donate them to Hal's House of Mirrors on the corner.

(First Love)

Dear Beautiful Mind,

I've been thinking,
perhaps we should
see other people.
It's feeling a bit
tight, like, you be…
you be…you be Me.
Frankly, Beautiful
Mind, you're
crampin'
my
style.
I think… I think.
I think… I think.
I think it's time,
time I jump a high,
new-wave, a poly-
amorous train, cut a
little deeper into my
whole-being buffet.
Get down with my
Bad Self, with my
wild old friends,
Body, Heart, and
Soul. We can talk
more about this
later if you want.
Well, maybe…
maybe not.
No. We will not.
Oh! My beloved

Beautiful Mind,
you will always
be my first.

(Queen for a Day)

By the time I arrived after changing all the lightbulbs on the farm, the beekeeper was sitting alone in the sun, legs up upon a low, heavy table, arms cradling his fuzzy head. His face, gently hooked nose, deep swim of eyes, his face at easy rest. And while the bees slept the psalm of his father's father's father, he turned to me and said, "I'm old. Sweetheart, I'm old."

He said he was old, but that yesterday, he'd bought his first guitar, his fiftieth, he said.

Then he took her out of her deerskin sheath and the still-sleeping bees crept from their honey dome home, their sturdy comb, to swarm his shoulders and chest. His fingers buzzing, cupping a long-fretted neck, curling round to firm-lift-press. And in this way, he configured a song. One hundred watts of incandescent wisdom. Exaltation. The apitoxin that sleeps at the base of his neck.

"I'm old."

White sage burning, he billowed new melody from his once hooded head, calling inside to the heartbeat of the hive, to a melt of fitted fear, six-sided cells of knowing. Calling inside to transform, chords, round at first, then bending sharp, clunking to his cool, ever-exposed toes with hesitation, lilting, then climbing back up all that came before.

A pheromone release breaking the air.

"Come. Everyone!"

Dry brine of thirty thousand lives ringing his warrior memory with hope and dread, salting his once daily bread.

"I'm."

Fingers following the release of the bees, stinging and singing, flowers, the breeze, to reveal a mysterious tongue, the resonance of an ever-present one and a new firm-lift-press.

Pluck. *Strum.* Roll.

Roll, roll, roll. Firm. Lift. Press.

His first. His fiftieth.

While the bees wept to cleanse. While the bees, they wept to cleanse.

(Nightlight)

I wish I could
climb to the top of your
mountain and stand silent and long,
holding my feet stone, to root your
river's bed, to slide your thoughts,
beliefs, ideals and fears
cascading
from your
beating head.
Empty high search
your eyes. Mine.
Your tide.
Your rise.
Foundation questions.
Shadow quake. I wish.
I could. Flow. Clear waters.
Reflecting inner glow. Opportunity
window possibility.
Sheeting veils
of snow.
Your mountaintop.
My flag.
Planted.
Removed.
Slippery hole
brushed gently closed.

(True North)

Clouds,
feathery, lofty, bright,
each moment
moving
beyond ideas
and mind.

Driving
into
the
sun.

(Ladder Day Saints)

When the knock came upon my door, I was in the kitchen making Sustainable Soup. Although I usually start my soup with onions and bay, today I was adding a bit of everything. Just a tiny bit.

And so, I carved off a ragged piece of yesterday's happiness, dry now at the edges, cut a thin slice of looming frustration from the air, cracked into a case of opportunity.

Dash, pour, pinch. I stirred it all together with whole-shouldered strokes, mixing in a few afterthoughts and a small handful of earth. Spicing it up with a twist of wild abandon.

Snipping in a few leaves of elation, I tripped across the room to grab a speck of dry fear and a second variety of long reaching roots. Fresh confidence.

Back and forth from the fridge, the cupboards, the garden, my mind. Dark sleepy vaults of all that is and is not.... Oops, where's the absolute? I thought I had some.

"Guess I'll try the neighbors," I said to no one in particular.

Washing my hands clean, I stepped into the early morning sun to meet two women in good simple shoes rolling a bulky case up my front walk.

"Hello! We are here. We have the answers," they said, only when they spoke the sound came out like this: "*Amasa. Ahuyama. Saguriko losi.*" I knew what they meant, but when I responded, "*Rutano lo huan. Sas. Lo doh inta se,*" I surprised myself. ("I'm not looking for answers," I said.)

They proceeded to open their case, spilling out stairways, ladders, and shelf upon shelf of heavy, ornate books. I understood now why they wore such shoes.

The first woman explained to me that it didn't matter what it was I sought; they had the answers. They could for sure assure me.

I told them, "*Agusani wala rotisana.*" ("I'm okay with mystery.") "*Ajini wuta mo lagunda. Lo insuta so.*" ("I believe in the goodness of death.")

The second woman immediately jumped up a ladder, slid a few panels, and thrust a large book in my hand. I took it and held it to my heart. From inside appeared a jade and onyx bird, who, instead of flying away, took her place upon my head. The women gasped. "*Shaou....*"

Suddenly, my cat appeared, black silky white, and wove herself between six steady legs, curling into a seamless ball. And with her satisfied sounds, a ladder came down upon her tail and a book upon the bird (my head). The women dropped to their knees. And in one more beat, the cat, the bird and I flew away, high above the neat white fence and trees, far beyond the absolute of my neighbors' yard.

(Land Ho)

Be your own freakin' beacon of light.
Steady swell, rage of wave.
Rise above to stand. Bare island tall.

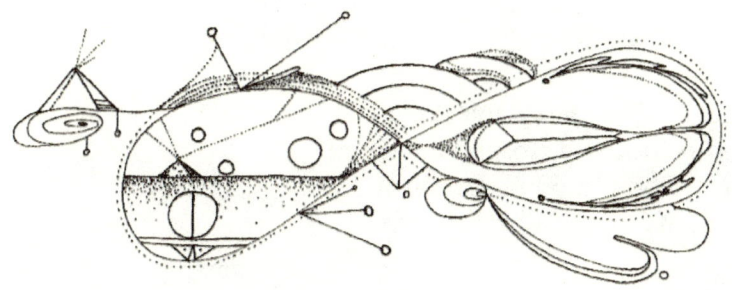

(Bells)

I saw you stop to pick a flower
outside the convenience store.
Buzz of both ways blowing your
hair straight to Heaven as you
bent to a deep-yellow reminder.

Bent to the stretch of sage grass
dunes your childhood camped out
on. Thin, smooth, pale grey sticks
dry-vine-tenting your fire, roasting
you whole. I saw you, but you
didn't see me, and we smiled.

You, there, bending to the first
time you lost yourself to a warm
roam of tongue in your ear, curious
waves rising your neck to no return.

I saw you, but you didn't
see me and we smiled.

Fuchsia bright, sticky-sweet bloom,
tucked behind the crossroads where
we once stood, holding hands in
support of our invisible bridge.

Tall pines of our steady
neighborhood ringing
our moment, echoing
the streets with change.

(Cybersack)

Soul Dealers, Inc.
Re: Two for One "Identity" Special

To Whom It May Concern:

After I filled my cart and put in the "TWOFER" promo code, a box flashed on the screen saying this offer was no longer available in my area.

It said I could have the *Lifetime Guarantee* instead, but I don't want that.

I want a pile on the floor I can step on.

(The trunk at the foot of my bed hasn't been opened in years. Last night I smashed the hinges off. Rust flew. I kept my eyes closed.)

Would you please honor the code I saw in the high flyin' magazine over Cairo, Bogotá, Hanoi, Paris? The one that says we can trade in our ideal standards and threadbare masks for an infinity pool, an all-you-can-eat, silk napkin buffet, a red, orange, yellow, green and blue slushy-bar array of SELF?

I know your *Lifetime Guarantee*. It's bunk, and should be abandoned. One star.

Sincerely,

"Baby Houdini Rocks"

(Politica)

Because you threaten me
and my hope for justice and equality,
I spit in your eye, only not really. Really,
I just bemoan you, over and over.
It's just like this. For so long now. Because
You're stubborn and righteous, and so am I
and I've been afraid of you for so long now.

I dream of a better world,
a world without the likes of you.

I'm so angry at you for all your hatred,
your bullying, your carelessness.
Your greed.

So angry.
So hungry.

My distance orbiting yours.
Yours orbiting mine.

If we made an omelet together,
who would crack the first egg?

Fully contained.

Where would it come from?
Would we have to cross the road?

Did you hear that tree
that may or may not
have fallen in the woods?

I'm hungry.

So hungry.

The butter is melting now,
foaming before our tired eyes,
tiny little brown bubbles of
Willingness. Spreading. Rising.

Eggs broken open,
whisked together....

Salt
and
pepper.

Yes.

Yes. Yes. Yes. Yes. *Yes.*

(Koan-Oh)

A flood passed through our hallway this morning, hot chocolate brown and foamy, rising to the chins of our family portraits, swirling cinnamon bark and coffee debris, though smelling of things waylaid. Standing beside the forward rush, piqued by remembrance, I felt the need to rip open a bag of biscotti with slivered almonds and offer it to the moment. To light a Turkish cigarette.

Standing then, smoke snaking, upon the banks of the widening wave, clutching a gold foil bag to my chest, I exhaled 200 decades of simmer and waited for a gondola to appear.

"Hell. It's not a place you go, but something you carry around with you."

Unpacking my bags, I practiced not waiting beside the hands of the clock, inhaling myself a mountain, TICK, exhaling myself a... TOCK. Hot chocolate brown overflow. Heaven waving non-waiting. TICK. Waving unpacked bags. TOCK.

When the gondola arrived, it was captainless and full of Grace. Diving aboard in my gold foil hat, I surfaced to shout, "Sing sweet! Sing low." And we did. The boat, the flood, Grace, and I passing through the pointed archway of these ancestral halls into jungles of steaming chaos, mystery space, red and blue spiral-painted trees not at all marking the way. Purple and white onion-domed homes glittering the now and the coming of night. New roads peeking from *tira-mi-su* clouds.

"Hell. It's not a place you go...."

When a fluffy pigeon appeared on the bow wearing open-toed rainbow shoes, I knew it was time to pull up the ladder and ascend, rise from this boat of *Do, Re, Mi* and pluck every string with blind fingertips. To trust every dream. To strum and feed our ease. Strum and feed, strum and feed, so we may burst with true-sweet need.

And to wash our seeds of suffering, smoke snaking, sticky froth. To wash our seeds of suffering and smile a lighted candle. Wash, smooth, feed. Unpack. Softly crack. While one hand reaches deep within to create new sound.

Clappk.

Klap. *Klapppk.* Clappp.

(Low Battery)

Dear Dopamine,

I thought you weren't
moving out 'til next month.
I'll have to keep your half of
the deposit, you know.

Sorry you feel so unfulfilled,
that onward-upward
is your one and only
spice of life.

It was great at first, though, right?
All that flyin' high was for real, right?
Sure did feel amazing.

I thought you liked
my fast mind,
my chocolate cake.
Tanqueray and tonic.
Tuesday's bargain basement.

Maybe if I change my "brand?"
My Facebook pic?
Smell of new leather?
Expand my horizons....
Maybe then you'll want me again.

I thought
it was
going good.

What?

You need more?

MORE. MORE. MORE.

Bing. Ping. BUZZ. *Flash!*
BING!
There ya go!
BING! BING!
YEA!!

"YEA!" Right?

Right?!?
RIGHT?!?!

(Take A Number)

I went to the new market behind the old redemption center, next to a rising lavender field, and the man behind the counter in his starchy whites and red rubber clogs surprised me.

"Patience?" he said, smiling brightly, Superman curl set low between two deeply set green eyes. "Acceptance?" "Vulnerability?"

"Flow?" I asked.

"Flow it is. How much?"

I said 66 pounds and laughed. He laughed, too, wrapping me in an invisible flannel blanket that smelled like hay. For a moment, I was off my feet.

"Okay, make it two," I said.

He started slicing, but it looked a little thick, so I stopped him. He laughed again. When he held it up, I could see the light.

"Oh. Okay," I said.

He let it fall all over, curling and piling, heaping and building. I was twitching a little. How was it going to fit in my bag? I said nothing, remembering a naughty song my cousin taught me in third grade. I thanked him.

Then I ran into an old friend. She was buying 12 pounds of courage. She took it thick. We decided to go to lunch.

Tinkling glasses and cool jazz. Our waitress said they had a special on Venus and Mars. I took both and ordered a side of chaos, not too spicy, please.

While waiting, I took the flow out of my bag and unwrapped it. It smelled divine, like clean winter toes dipping into a warm bubbling spring. I lifted a piece and smoothed it out, crumpled it up, smoothed it out. Then I began folding, 2,000 folds, transforming it into a *Morigami* crane. My friend and I then folded 8 billion more, joining each to the other with an obsidian tear and silken thread.

Later, we left them on our table for our server, who had accidently stumbled and spilled all of Venus and Mars upon me. I smiled at her then, took the upright side of chaos, squeezed on fresh lime and let slide.

(Date Line)

There was that time I loved you
when, walking together, you gave
me your hand. The pressure felt so
sure, as we took our first uneven steps.
As we dodged crusty sleeping dogs and
puddle-splashing motorbikes laden turmeric,
ginger, gold. Twin roosters, in trance, swaying
from the bend of our handlebar hold. There was
that time. High above the river's rush and thunder's
wide escape, you, ripping thru my chest, silk-wrapped
and bold. And me, and my child-awe, lapping up your
outpour of sky. I was another hemisphere then, another
found dimension, orbiting nothing but the reflection of
your warm sea, bobbing frond green. Finger-smeared
lenses filtering out your too-bright sun, painting us
amber rose. Slick city sidewalks bringing us to
our knees. Sand and small stones digging in with
glee. Digging into the abrasion of what would
come to be. We slid on, our open spread of
clay and heat, our "I'll be damned," our
coral reef. I loved you then. New lungs
believing in your soft, good air, your
wisteria, tangle-drape fall of hair.
Arms strong and curling a trans-
parent pearl embrace to blot
out and erase my carefully
crafted map. My persona.
My past, laid thick before
our tender swell,
our nakedness,
our ideal.

(Cascadence)

Dear Great Mystery,

On my way
walking to your
house, I tripped over a slick,
gnarled root and fell, fell hard,
to the nearby ground. I landed
atop a tiny snake. Well, I can tell you,
she felt pretty bombarded and reacted
back, biting my cool outstretched hand,
my broken advance, my far-reaching
plans. And then, I felt bombarded, so I
bit her back, grabbing hold her pointy
tail, stale of habit and yesterday's heat.
Camouflage. And together we began
to roll, together we formed a thin,
sweeping O. Bend of meadow,
steppe rust red. Until we landed
instead, a swirl of setting sun,
deep in the intimacy of your
brambly edge. Your (always
under renovation) Home
Sweet Home. Then, my
dear, we let go.

(Resurrection)

This morning, as the sun cracks the horizon, our new dawn rivaling the tenacity of the next door neighbor's French bulldog, woolen carpets growing ochre-deep ancestral corn up the wall, I turn to face the gap, chasm of birth that once ripped through, but today I see it differently.

Today I see it filling in. Today, I see that in between the rocks that separate rises an outreach of bright pale yellow-green. Palm-shaped, baby leaves of growth.

Yeah, it appears that a fire swept through here. Yeah, upon closer inspection, creosote rubble tumbling new skin of feet, I see a semblance of fine, black transformative ash dissolving to clear and feed.

I see the fire still here, ablaze in our human gap, arcing and diving and swirling a powerful magnificence to burn away and release all that lay stagnant, low, and painfully asleep. I see the black burning-orange of our past filling, filling in. And I turn then, to wash my face and spit, spit it all out to Earth's great, healing sink.

(You Can Bank on It)

Yesterday afternoon, I saw a hundred-dollar bill, folded in half, lying in the middle of the street. I looked around, saw no one, then went over and picked it up. A few feet away lay a second hundred-dollar bill. Still no cars, or pedestrians in sight, I took a large step, squatted down, and picked it up. Then I saw a third. Rubbing them together and into my palms, I did a little dance, looked to the sky, and returned home.

I decided to bury the bills in the back yard.

At first, I was having a hard time deciding where to bury them. Should I put them beside my first crush, or beneath my failed entrance exams? Maybe over next to Moxie, our childhood dog? Or under the time I accidentally set the neighbor's car on fire? Was there even any more room in this back yard? It used to be so organized, one side buried to hold onto, the other buried to transform, a sweet, tinkling stream down the center.

The stream dried up a decade ago. And now I couldn't really be sure of anything. I decided to try the northeast corner, next to where I thought I'd buried my debate team trophies.

I went to get the garden shovel, but couldn't find it. I supposed I'd have to use the shovel my great, great, great, great grandfather gave me, made of wagon wheels, buffalo teeth, and pride, with a tip of black diamond tears. Usually, I only used this for revelation, but today, it'd have to do.

I began digging and immediately hit rock. I moved a bit to the left and hit rock. I moved further left, hit rock. Just then an opossum dropped from the sky, nearly landing on my head. She was smoky blue and chartreuse, with a sleek pink tail. She turned slowly to look at me and said, *"Your perceptions are yours alone."*

I moved to the southwest corner.

Using the strength of all who'd come before, I plunged the ancient shovel to Earth.

I hit rock.

Dabbing cool sweat from my brow and sighing a colossal sigh, I wiped every story and half-story from the cradle of my weary tool, put the dusty bills in my pocket, and knelt to kiss the Earth.

(Lifeboat)

Wanna share a banana split?
I have a silver spoon in my bag
from long before you or I were born.

We can take turns. You start on
the strawberry side, ten million
promise seeds. And I'll go for
the *piña*, sweet golden pricks
and emerging eyes. Later,
we can meet in the hot fudge
center and feed each other
our cherry-topped divine.

Back and forth. Back and forth.
From my open mouth to yours,
your open mouth to mine.

And when we finish, we can wipe
our tool clean, tuck her back inside,
climb into our flimsy red-plastic
boat, and launch ourselves offshore.

If a big wave comes and threatens
to crash our heating heads, we can
both jump in front and push the
boat's nose down, dive deeply
under. Flow with the flood
and emerge on the other side
of all our windswept questions.

From there we can sun ourselves
upon the rocks, smooth with the

endless tide.
You. And I.
Full-bellied.
Splitting
ourselves
lengthwise.
One slow
bite at a
time.

(Stone Cold)

I think being a hypocrite with
awareness is one of the greatest
things to be. Cursing the neighbor's
vicious dog, as we sink our gleam of
fangs to a new ankle. Bemoaning the
oblong hole in our sock as we pull on
another day of choice, ideas of what's
right, acceptable. Pulling up to our knees
with comfort and assuredness of all that's
in between, all that is beyond. Smug smile.
"Look at you!" we say. Then, it's: "You are me."
Sitting at the rise behind the Seven Eleven, dull
rush knowing, peering upward, peering down,
eyes surfing familiar waves to land upon the
roiling smoke of a volcano top, distant at first.
An oblong, curious gap. Then, in an instant,
a flash of awareness, and there we are, up to
our knees in red hot lava. Blackened crust
forming over top, breaking open to pour
forth more. Standing knee deep in our
powerful, collective shit, pointing a long
dirty-nailed finger back to the star of
our own third eye, saying, "Look!
Look at you, socks pulled up.
Lava all around."

(Zzzen)

This mountain,
raw
compression,
seems unmoving,
but it is not.

(Caressence)

Please, let us return to
tenderness as much as
possible. When sly, wiry
hairs raise up a continental
divide, seeping heart, black
strap slow, twisting a course
of two-faced veins, let there be
a remembrance of oxygen. Let
us breathe in through bare feet
a composted constellation,
solid, liquid, gas, of all that
has broken us. Tight lungs
awakening to the scents
of abandon, rejection and
ignorance to mingle the
steaming pile of our half
cracked seeds and bitter
peelings, our empty shells
and grinds, heating from
inside to rise, to dust a
deep summer sky and
recycle out to star
sparking lines. To
a full-on-gorgeous
caress, fleshed out
with patience
and time.

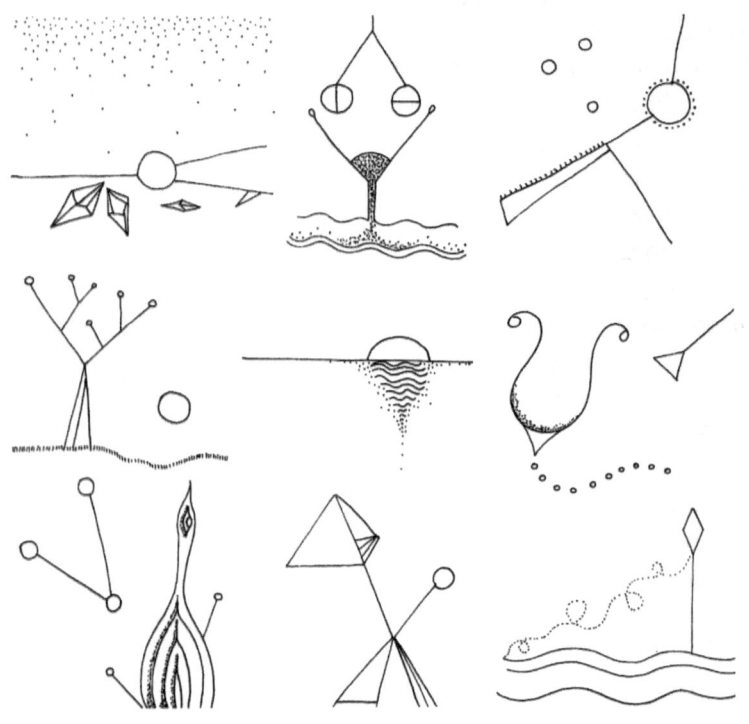

(Welcome Mat)

Dear Limitations,

Please, excuse me.
While you sat on the back porch,
crystal sweat scratching your
sunburned neck, legs outstretched,
knees buzzing surrender, I was lost in
a ten-mile pile of dirty pots and pans,
washing, scrubbing, chipping away
all the caked-on-shit of yesterday.

I didn't even offer you a glass of water.

I just had to transform
that shameful mess.
You know, keep on going.
By lunchtime, my hands were
pale swollen prunes, clumsy
with insistence. My shoulders
stooped with myopic craze.

If only I'd invited you in,
taken a seat in a straight-
backed chair before you,
massaged your dirty feet.

Thank you so much for coming.
I really was happy to see you.
Though maybe next time
we could head toward
your place instead,
leave this precious story

to soak for a while.

Feed each other take-
out in the park instead.

(Same Wavelength)

I'll leave my house
in five minutes.
You do it, too.
And we'll meet halfway,
on the bridge,
over the rush of almost
freezing water,
flowing as it does
to go where it goes.
If your hands get cold,
you can use one
of my mittens.
Two hands
in one.

(Lowdown)

Make me a sandwich
of emptiness and trust
and I'll eat
like a king,
a lion,
the sun,
and until my last meal,
I'll lie,
feet up,
back softly curled,
within the hammock
of my soul,
holding the spanning
of this most ancient seed.

(Late Summer)

Dear Tenacity,

Ever since the state fair pie-eating contest,
things just haven't been the same between us.

I don't know if it was the butter/lard ratio
in that last crust, or perhaps the humidity
that caught your throat. Anyway, I'm sorry.

I miss you and I don't.

I'm halfway through *Les Misérables,*
and in October, I leave for an
eleven-day silent retreat.

Hope to hear from you soon….

(High Noon)

I'd already missed two appointments with the six-hundred-year-old clockmaker. Today, I was determined to make it to his grotto at the top of the village.

I figured I'd start out extra early, just before the sun rose over the sleeping cove, liquid hope taunting bare shoulders and toes. However, my alarm didn't go off. I'd been afraid of that, so for most of the night, I didn't sleep. Then, without knowing it, I fell fast into a vast technicolor maze.

When my cat, Stew, woke me by jumping on my head, I was crammed in a hot, windowless van of parka wearing Aborigines, teetering on a sandstone cliff, my young son at the wheel, his grandfather under the hood. Everyone laughing as we rocked back and forth, back and forth.

Shaking myself from the tumult of the dream, I dressed and ran to the well, drew up the thin wooden bucket and dashed a brand-new-day upon my face.

I'd decided to take the invisible staircase, avoid the chunky fittings of center Earth. About halfway up, I stopped in an arched doorway to ask for a drink. Peering inside, I could just make out a figure floating before a streaming loom. Hearing the bright chime of her ancestral bell, the old woman, Silver Crone, Purple Sage, *The Time Is Not Late*, beckoned me in. Where, upon *really* seeing me, she kissed me high upon both cheeks and wrapped my neck with thick, white, living fur.

Once adjusted to the inner foggy light, I saw a low table where a young raven moved, sorting precious memories and chanting in round. He was making piles, one seeping, one flaming, one leaden, one gold.... I reached out to touch the gold but drew back as the woman presented me with a swirling cup, an endless drink of clear. Wetting my soul and sighing out loud, I thanked her, turned on my heel, and bowed out. I had an appointment with a six-hundred-year-old clockmaker to keep.

After another sixteen yawns, I reached the top. I don't know why, but I was surprised by the face of the clock. It was as large as the world's superego, round as completion, sharp as false knowing, bejeweled with crowns and scepters, daggers and chains and cranking softly with a labored, mechanical breath.

Just as the clockmaker met me beneath the sole lemon tree, a large ebony cloud blew in from the west. We reached for one another then. And, as a clap of thunder gave way to a strike of bright light, the clock forever stopped its measured talk. Then, the maker, spirit and man, parted the wildness from my face, gazed deeply to my whole, and said, "Everything in its own time, dear heart. *Everything in its time.*"

(Amen)

I know you're here cuz the sun is
rising, just starting to spill and
the sounds that surround shift
from clanging and buzzing,
ripping and pounding to
gentler waves, misty yellow
gray. I know you're here cuz
the new sign upon the door is
in a simple language I can
understand. When I see this,
I take the unfamiliar, familiar
sign in my hands and turn it over
to check the other side. Written there,
"This is no new sign." Hanging it up
again, I enter the open door where
I take a seat, pause long, drop to
my knees, curl my toes, plant
my high forehead and breathe.
Tiny prancing roots of you
filling my being, dancing
my legs, arms, hips and
head. Filling me up.
Purifying me
from within.

(Year Abroad)

Do you remember the time
you fed me Parmesan and pear,
golden as the Tuscan sun? When
we picked bare feet between cool
marble stones, careful not to disturb
endless, flowered sleep? When we
looked and looked, finding nowhere
to pee? And then, a tiny-soft, sea-
speckled-brown bird fell from a
crowded, sagging bough, wing
bent and hanging, and we
wrapped her in your pale
blue shirt and we took her
home, feeding her warm
soulful drops of your
childhood until
she could fly,
fly again.

(Preface)

I'm tearing the cover off this old book. It smells too musty. Perhaps I should burn it. Nah, I think I'll hang it outside instead, naked and flapping its yellowed paper wings to the sound of a new beat. A new beat coming from up over the hill. From up over the hill. Hey! I can see *really* far from here. 360°. Hey, yeah, I'm tearing the cover off this old, encaustic book.

(Who You Callin' Dwarf?)

Outside my bedroom window, Pluto stops to tie her shoe. Already the roosters had awakened me, coughing their black, iridescent feather-flags to float the streets of change. Possibility.

I'd come to quickly, my body sensing the silent horns of this new, wily wave, this creeping, planetary invade.

Pluto had perhaps had too much to drink. Half sitting, half standing beneath the datura tree, burlap sash loose at the knees, tomorrow's fedora cocked lightly upon her swirling head, she was having a lot of trouble with her shoes. Platform sneakers elevating her while coolly weighing her down. Blossoms of the moon-kissed tree reflecting shadowy dreams upon her already darkened face.

I heard her curse. "Fuck," she said. Then she spit, gravel and dust of six trillion lifetimes, toward the expanding base and coiling roots of us. Spit upon Earth's humanity. Upon our knowing, our not-knowing. Our not not-knowing.

Approaching her from the south, sphinxlike in my new silk pajamas, I said, "Yes," and we saw one another then.

Her endless spiral embracing my imagined, private escape and shaking it raw. Her renegade waltz taking hold my own. The two of us entwining energies, transforming fate. Smooth hand of eternity flicking winds of change, fanning the flame, calling me to surrender, deeply explore, be brave.

"Good Mourning," Pluto said, half smiling, reaching out a bare arm to caress my cheek. My see-through grief. Then, kicking clunky shoes to the curb, she swept me in to her tight, slippery chest, icy crystals, newfound space.

And in that moment, I knew I could never let go.

I knew....

"Good Mourning," I said, arching my back to kiss her glittery head. "Good Mourning.

"I know.

"I know.

"I know.

"I know I do not know."

Then, shivering yesterday's anticipation, brought back by the warmth of my true breath, I let go.

I let let go.

Let go... all I do not know, and fell asleep, naked, alone and flat on my back, beneath a night-blooming tree.

(Tank Half Full)

I had a dream you
and I were riding
turtles in a southern
sea, only then your
turtle turned into a squid
and I got lost in a spray of
jet black. At those depths,
It took a little while for it to
clear. Then I remembered
about "the bends" and got
scared, grabbed hold of
a dolphin ping instead.
Way ahead. Electric blue
of us pulsating through
a vast and ancient sea.
Echolocation,
something
to trust.

(DIY)

Someone stepped on my toes
in line at the grocery store and
didn't say they were sorry. Boxes
of dry, clattery stuff pushing
forward, invading my space,
conveying convenience,
crossing the line of my
black plastic bar.
When I turned around in
scorn, I pulled an old muscle
in my hip. Seeing no one behind,
no one before, my toes spread wide.
So wide I stepped on them again. Bit my
tongue. Grabbed some organic sugar-free
mints in a snowflake magic-palace tin and
climbed, pick-axing mind, to the top, did an
upward dog, bark-barked out loud, raised
my leg and fell-down upon my face. Upon
my wrinkled remembrance. My fog of
gratitude. The smiling cashier gave
me a treat anyway and I tossed it,
overhead, to a guy in line, who
caught it high. "Good boy!"
"Good boy!" he said.

(Check Your Mail)

Dear Passion,

It seems that while you were deeply kissing in the streets of Ibiza, cliff diving to Jupiter and Mars, slathering cool ambergris upon red-hot-coal washed feet, you may have missed my note.

I've put in a change of address.

You can reach me now,
anytime, anywhere:

My Beating Heart,
Poste Restante

(Ave Maria)

Just after sunset, if you take the back way toward Plaza Mea Culpa, avoiding Harbinger Alley and Point Atrocity, you'll find a rickety stand set up, where a speechless man with no arms or legs will offer to tie your shoelaces together for a song. Literally, for a song, he'll take all the blame for you when you fall.

Of course, I went for it. "Tie me up, sir. Yes, please."

First, I sang Piaf's "Non, Je Ne Regrette Rien," and though the maestro didn't speak, he laughed. He laughed until rainbow stars came out of his robust chest. He laughed until all the hairs of all the people in all the world stood at joyful attention, just for a second, then lay themselves back down, hissing softly, "*Mea Culpa. Mea Culpa.*" Then, when he went to tie my long bootlaces together, he took them out instead.

Quickly they flew away to a nearby tree, the entire tree a nest of sighing, moaning laces. Tied together, and not, they flew high, they flew low. Inside, and out.

Without my laces, my feet slid from my heavy boots. In my thin-stockinged feet I walked slowly to the base of the tree, leaned every bit of my quilted self against it. Squares of silky orange and green misunderstanding. Jagged scraps of sapphire pain. Amber-pink heat of delight. And while I swooned and hugged the tree, my abandoned weight, my boots, started walking, then dancing, circles in front of the beautiful man. His pregnant laughter moving from stars to sweet tears.

He invited me to join the circle dance, but I was already halfway up the tree, arms wide. I could see my own thick laces weaving themselves deeper in, weaving themselves through the pulse and reflection of our nest.

When a carpet began to appear from within the parting sea, in the highest bough of the tree, I was hardly surprised. It grew and grew, my quilted bits weft to the collective warp, then finally, we sprang free.

We sprang free.

Laying prone, feet dangling behind, cobra-crane neck, I took a long, smooth ride, leaving Mea Culpa square and its knots behind. Raising myself up, long supple spine, to the smile of every face, to a newfound grace, to take my first break, just up ahead, Toda Vista Lane.

(Next Exit)

My feet were hurting as I
climb-climbed your mountain,
so I sat down, let you rub them instead.

(Next to Godliness)

Dear Presence,

Oh, that smile!
Strolling slowly
all over early morning town.
Nothing to sweep up here,
nothing to brush through,
comb over, or wet down.
Sun-kissed contentment
slung across your deep
brown face.
Divine wisdom,
undeclared.
Slung across.
As if innate
spiritual
freedom
is a Goddamn
Real Thing. Oh!
Thank you.

Thank you.
Thank you.
Thank you,
for always
walking shirtless,
feet bare,
for never
waiting
for what
comes
next.

(Preheated)

I made muffins for you.
First, I whisked the shit out of
everything you were ever told
about separation, competition,
and achievement. Then I melted
the fear of a lifetime in a heavy-
bottomed pan and gently blended
it in, slowly lifting-up from the bottom,
up and over, turning full, smooth circles
of willingness. Once the emulsion of these
had set, I let it rest for a while upon the
back deck. It started raining, a warm rain.
After a few hours, I added your first true
heartbreak. Unfortunately, I'd forgotten to
defrost it, so I had to improvise. I grated
it up with an ancient fine-toothed tool and
sprinkled it carefully over the top. Next
came two cups of hard rejection. Dump.
Dump. And a long, sweet pour of hope.
Three heaping spoons of "Hell, yes!"
and a dash each of pluck and humility,
stirred until barely blended. I worked
quickly then...moving toward the final
transformation, low, steady heat. I'd decided
to use those frilly baking papers, pink polka-
dots, so I wouldn't have to wash the pan. The
muffins rose beautifully, cracking perfect,
golden-brown domes. Thirteen in all. If you're
around later, my friend, I can make coffee, too.

(Song of Cosmic Remembrance)

I wanted to invite the pelicans to my party, but I figured they'd feel claustrophobic, maybe make a big mess. Yesterday, when I sat up on the rocks overlooking the endless forces of saltwater and sky and they passed by, powerful wings lifting lines of synchronicity and ease, I knew I needed them at my party. I needed them.

I called to them, but they didn't hear me. I tried again, both in English and Spanish, then in Indonesian, just to be sure. When one dipped down and to the side to dodge an incoming wave, so did the next, the next, the next. They did so as One. Pure connectedness flying by.

No way did they hear me in my feeble, plying cry.

I turned then to the setting sun and began to sing softly until the sky of my soul streamed from my eyes. Silent, gentle tears rolling feathery down the folded map of me. Rolling to the tips of my new beginnings, to the jagged rocks of me and eighteen billion others. All of us in our melting need, a rush of great, gushing seeds to feed the brilliant, bucket-mouthed birds within. All of us flying spacious above this ravenous Earth Party, pouring down our intergalactic truth. Opening ourselves to the fluid acquaintance of a whale, blue with being. Blue with being and everything.

(And Then Some)

Spread a little more joy
on your bread this morning!
Go ahead, wash your face in it.
Wrap it round your waist. Put it
in a vase. Sweep it to the streets.

(Slow Drip)

Dear Humanity,

Pour yourself another cup of insight.
I brewed it super strong this season.

Sorry for the heavy intensity
outside your window this morning,
burnished taillights of retrograde
karmic lord Saturn and shady Pluto
looping close, illuminating
stale chinks in your foundation,
heating the primordial mirror
of your dawn.

There's a ladder in the garden.
If you want, you can climb
up to get a fresh view.
(The plants will show
you the way. The plants
will show you the way.)

The meeting of
the Compassion for
Assholes Collective starts in ten.

We've asked Higher Mind and Open
Heart to co-facilitate. The collective is
spiral shaped, thirty-three million,
three hundred thirty-three
members so far. Not too bad.

To join, you don't have to be
an asshole, per se, just act
like one sometimes. It's
the compassion part
that can be tricky.

Go on then, take a seat,
make yourself comfortable.
If you're chilly, you can
put on someone else's
shoes. There's also a
couple hypo-
allergenic
shawls
behind
the door.
Forgiveness
and Grace.

We're so pleased you're here.

With Love
and Light,

The Universe

(Morphosis)

Be your own shaman.
May breath be your guide.
Inhale yourself a swinging vine.
Exhale yourself wetted cheeks.
Know yourself a mountain peak.
Inhale yourself bright purple pain.
Exhale yourself needed rain.
Be your own shaman.
Be your own guide.
Inhale yourself
beyond divide.
Exhale yourself...
and you will find....
Nothing is static.
All is divine.

(Celestial Yes)

There are those days when everything fits
despite the inner bruise of fruit
or sharp elbow of a cop,
when a simple arch
of brown stone
takes hold
a buzz
zing
heart
bringing
her to open
reception and
the bloom of a
Christmas cactus
in early June. Those
days when brick-oven
domes churn out crisp,
warm love, steaming
the streets clean of
question. Heavenly
footfalls, lost horizons
adrift on a briny wake.
There are those days. Those
days when everything fits, deep
like the curved, elastic corners of
sunshiny sheets tucked under
tired skin, sweated and dried.
Perfect days when all we need
is a slender slice of everyday,
anyway, come-what-may sky.

Thank you.

You are welcome.

www.ingramcontent.com/pod-product-compliance
Lightning Source LLC
Chambersburg PA
CBHW021957290426
44108CB00012B/1108